SIDNEY CROSBY

BY RYAN NAGELHOUT

 Gareth Stevens
PUBLISHING

Please visit our website, www.garethstevens.com. For a free color catalog of all our high-quality books, call toll free 1-800-542-2595 or fax 1-877-542-2596.

Library of Congress Cataloging-in-Publication Data

Names: Nagelhout, Ryan, author.
Title: Sidney Crosby / Ryan Nagelhout.
Description: New York : Gareth Stevens Publishing, [2017] | Series: Sports
  MVPs | Includes index.
Identifiers: LCCN 2016007215 | ISBN 9781482446463 (paperback) | ISBN
  9781482446432 (library bound) | ISBN 9781482446326 (6 pack)
Subjects: LCSH: Crosby, Sidney, 1987–Juvenile literature. | Hockey
  players–Canada–Biography–Juvenile literature.
Classification: LCC GV848.5.C76 .N36 2017 | DDC 796.962092–dc23
LC record available at http://lccn.loc.gov/2016007215

Published in 2017 by
Gareth Stevens Publishing
111 East 14th Street, Suite 349
New York, NY 10003

Copyright © 2017 Gareth Stevens Publishing

Designer: Samantha DeMartin
Editor: Ryan Nagelhout

Photo credits: Cover, pp. 1, 21 (Stanley Cup) Gregory Shamus/National Hockey League/Getty Images; p. 5 Brian Bahr/Getty Images Sport/Getty Images; pp. 7, 11 Dave Sandford/Getty Images Sport/Getty Images; p. 9 Claus Anderson/Getty Images Sport/Getty Images; pp. 13, 15, 19 Bruce Bennett/Getty Images Sport/Getty Images; p. 17 Andre Ringuette/National Hockey League/Getty Images; p. 21 (trophies) Incomible/Shutterstock.com.

Printed in the United States of America

CPSIA compliance information: Batch #CS16GS: For further information contact Gareth Stevens, New York, New York at 1-800-542-2595.

CONTENTS

Boldface words appear in the glossary.

Sid the Kid

Sidney Crosby is a hockey superstar. He's the captain of the Pittsburgh Penguins, a Stanley Cup **champion**, and an Olympic hero in Canada. He has scored big goals and won **trophies** for his team and his country. How much do you know about "Sid the Kid"?

Born in Canada

Crosby was born on August 7, 1987, in Cole Harbour, Nova Scotia, Canada. His dad taught him how to play hockey. He shot hockey pucks at an old clothes dryer in his basement. He learned to skate when he was 3!

7

To Minnesota

Crosby played minor hockey in Canada growing up. In 2002, he moved to Faribault, Minnesota, to attend Shattuck-St. Mary's **boarding school**. He played hockey there for one year. In 2003, Crosby was **drafted** first overall by Rimouski Océanic of the Quebec Major Junior Hockey League (QMJHL).

Top Pick

Crosby played two seasons with Rimouski in the QMJHL. In 2005, he was drafted first overall by the Pittsburgh Penguins in the National Hockey League Entry Draft. He played center for the Penguins right away. He scored 102 points his first year in the NHL!

The Hat Trick

In 2007, Crosby led the Penguins to the playoffs. He became the youngest winner of the Art Ross Trophy, given to the NHL's top scorer. He also won the Lester B. Pearson **Award** and the Hart Memorial Trophy. These trophies are given to the league's most valuable player (MVP)!

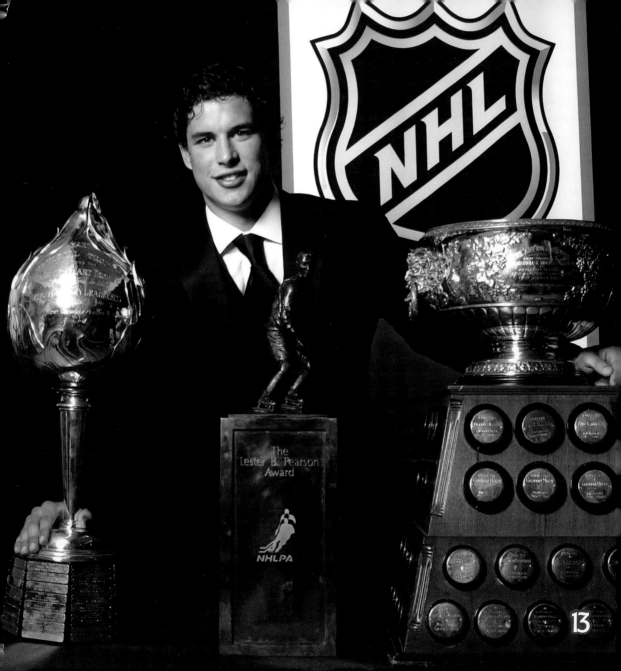

The Lester B. Pearson Award

NHLPA

13

Captain and First Finals

Crosby was named Pittsburgh's captain after the 2007 season. In 2008, Crosby led the Penguins to the Stanley Cup Finals. They lost to the Detroit Red Wings. The two teams met in the finals the next season. This time, the Penguins won!

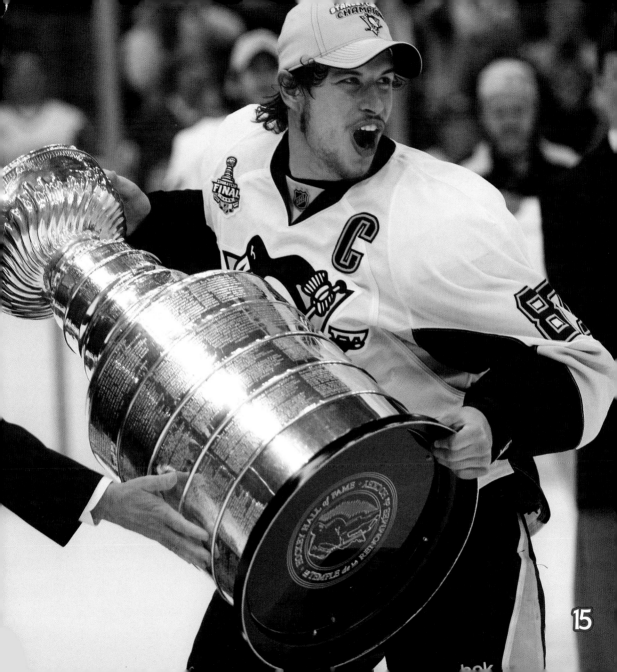

Stanley Cup Champs

Crosby missed parts of the next two seasons with head **injuries**. In the 2010–2011 season, he only played in 41 games. But he still led the Penguins in scoring! In 2013, he won the Ted Lindsay Award. It was the new name for the Lester B. Pearson Award, which he had won in 2007.

Kid Canada

In 2005, Crosby won gold with Canada in the U-18 World Juniors Ice Hockey Championships. He has also played for Team Canada in the Olympics. Crosby scored in **overtime** in the gold medal game against the United States in 2010. He won gold again at the Olympics in 2014.

More Awards

In 2014, Crosby won his second Art Ross and Hart Memorial Trophies. He also won a third Ted Lindsay Award. Crosby and the Penguins won the Stanley Cup again in 2016. He also won the playoff MVP award—the Conn Smythe!

TROPHY CASE

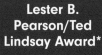

Lester B. Pearson/Ted Lindsay Award*
2006–2007
2012–2013
2013–2014

Olympic Gold Medal
2010 2014

Maurice Richard Trophy
2009–2010

Stanley Cup Champion 2009 2016
Conn Smythe Award 2016

Art Ross Trophy
2006–2007   2013–2014

Hart Memorial Trophy
2006–2007   2013–2014

* award was renamed in 2010

GLOSSARY

award: a prize given to someone

boarding school: a school where students live

champion: the overall winner of something

draft: to pick players for a team. Also, the act of picking players for a team.

injury: hurt or loss to the body

overtime: an extra period of time needed to find a game's winner

trophy: a prize given for winning or doing something notable

FOR MORE INFORMATION

BOOKS

Burgan, Michael. *Sidney Crosby*. North Mankato, MN: Capstone Press, 2015.

Graves, Will. *The Best Hockey Players of All Time*. Minneapolis, MN: ABDO Publishing, 2015.

Nagle, Jeanne. *Sidney Crosby: One of the NHL's Top Scorers*. New York, NY: Britannica Educational Publishing, 2016.

WEBSITES

Sidney Crosby
hockey-reference.com/players/c/crosbsi01.html
Find more of Crosby's stats and awards here.

Sidney Crosby Hockey School
sidneycrosbyhockeyschool.com
Find out more about the hockey school Crosby runs every summer.

Publisher's note to educators and parents: Our editors have carefully reviewed these websites to ensure that they are suitable for students. Many websites change frequently, however, and we cannot guarantee that a site's future contents will continue to meet our high standards of quality and educational value. Be advised that students should be closely supervised whenever they access the Internet.

INDEX